Published by Nauset Press

nausetpress.com

Wareham, MA

Cover and Book Design: Nauset Press.

Cover Photo: Copyright © 2020 Hendy.mp/Shutterstock. No use without permission.

Author Photo: Copyright © 2022 Carolyn Monastra

ISBN: 979-8-9859692-2-1

Library of Congress Control Number: 2022915391

CROWDED
BETSY ANDREWS

In remembrance:

Joseph John Andrews

August 11, 1928 – April 8, 2015

Today, for the first time in human history, the human race, collectively, is mourning for a dying planet. The fate of the earth depends upon our understanding the dynamics of the mourning process. Though it is tempting to lament the fate of the earth and blame our forebears for its present state, we must put these childish sentiments aside and take up the adult task of re-visioning our ancestral inheritance and educating the dead.

— Greg Mogenson, *Greeting the Angels: An Imaginal View of the Mourning Process*

CONTENTS

MAN IN FLIGHT

My father, lungs a-warble, spreads his arms on the nursing home bed,

swoops low over rough, unfamiliar terrain. The hospice nurse ticks off procedures.

My mother signs papers with her large, lush loops, so ravishing,

more ravishing than the chicken-scratch scrawl of my father's hand,

clubbed now, a long-lost claw—phylogenesis recapitulated, and ontogenesis, too.

Overhead, the geese tootle toward the marsh.

They're rolling the old folks into the commons, lining them up before the TV.

I look out the window. The geese have landed,

foraging slowly on the manicured lawn, unruffled, for now,

by organochlorides and organophosphates and their amplification

in the rat-a-tat, rat-a-tat blood of a bird. *And 2 and 4 and 2 and 4*,

my father's bent language its own looping code, laying an egg like a parrot,

and every so often an *embarrassed embarrassed* and every so often a *dammit*.

"Our relationship wasn't exactly warm and fuzzy," my mother blinks

behind drugstore specs. They make her look owlish.

She isn't owlish; she's ravishing, more ravishing than ever she was

back in the days when the couch was her tether and pills were her hood

and my father flew at her with razor blades lashed to his feet.

The hospice nurse ticks off further procedures.

The geese crop the grass; their idyll won't last. The city, half-cocked,

is gunning for them, hatching a brood of lethal procedures

to rid itself of the soft, light bodies so hazardous to man in flight.

CROWDED

Oh finches of the plastic feeder in your incomparable yellow in the April damp,

is there room enough on the porch rail beside you for his tiny feet to clamp

like Channellocks, to cinch like a workshop grip? The rotting handrail greasy with shit,

is there space here to fit his vroom-vroom breast, his toylike dragon paws?

Claws bared to the epoch, the torn shopping bags fan their tails in the branches

like paradise's birds in opulent expulsion, cast out into nowhere and kinging it.

Noahs of the skies, they neither live nor die, but in ever-diminishing arks, multiply;

immortality an ethylene monomer chain, the new world born again and again

on the trillion-times mien of convenience. Oh finches. Shove over.

This great heart is assembled yet incomplete, let his grasping feet clench here,

let his shadow retreat from gravity's rail-and-spike danger, the anger that entraps him

unfurling and swirling in the haze, its lethal electrical double-width fence smelted for feeders

where miniscule dragons can gobble their fill, and on the shrill get-get-get of the finches' example,

sample lift in the consoling dark where the searchlights park, having licked their sharp teeth

and cut engines. And me? On the ground here, finches, wobbling towards the scope,

with the hope of sighting elfin reptilian wings on the move, a thing proven true enough for wanting

Up here on the spot-lung mountaintop, the dragon inside the body caves in,

bony beak haggles like a bellows for air, like a pocket that's sighing for change.

The coal tunnel throat gulps burnt and sour, the char in a barrel of blasted fish,

a wheezing canary's final wish for wings in sunlight, like smack in a vein that's collapsing

while gravity's railroad takes its glum lumps from the childhood heaps at Carbondale

to the childhood mules on the D&H Canal along 16 miles of hand-hammered tracks,

the stuttering slump of a dragon's racked back, the blap-blap-blap fist in his war chest gunning

against its cage; a family bound to gravity by rage, down and panting on the living room rug,

a 4-year-old hugging her knees. Can't we please bolt the door on the afterworld of love?

A bird will eat from a still hand, dragon; lie down in the brownfields, disarmed

Tiny dragon, the dragonflies wonder at your disparate eyes, oblivion and heaven in one reckless face,

Neptune and mythical Venus erasing the present, time and again, tiny dragon there and not there

when he hangs in the shit-and-coal stinking air rummaging in the trash, a starling among starlings

murmuring rash, self-interested things, a ne'er-may-care in a junk heap of wings

fire-fueled and weaving all over the road, singing along to the 8-track to keep himself from crashing

Fly me to the moon, let me play among the stars, let me see what spring is like on Jupiter and Mars

Such is our era and so is our fashion. Are we through yet with the analogy of the boiling toad?

We're not gradual; we'll unload our ammo—whammo!—in a minute,

scorch the whole planet if there's something for us in it. What cruelty we've dealt

the earth's routine trust, bird in a cage on a windowsill, chirping and blinking at the dust

So how in hell did we end up with dragon? Fly ash and cold pit and the long slip down,

the beast that summons then swallows the drooping, earth-gut town,

potatoes for breakfast and potatoes for supper and potatoes for lunch tomorrow,

a dragon's dragon's silica chest borrowing breath from a bottle of sorrow,

inheritance less a continuous guzzle than an accretion of sags and troughs,

the sorry mountainside giving in, heaving and wheezing, coughs;

then a bird's-eye view of oblivion from a ridge half-forgotten as heartbreak,

the body raked with incoming garbage: arsenic, lead, cadmium, chromium, iron, uranium, nickel,

hard little blue-gray assassins burrowed like fugitives under the skin,

that thin line between the hurt-borne self and a purple-hearted projection,

a Tin Man's chest full of nothing but pressure and wartime souvenirs; then years

of fragile delusion, a performance of the American dream underwritten by Standard Oil

with an excessively boozy intermission and a violent second act.

"He had tremendous hatred for a lot of women," my uncle interrupts.

"He didn't have the nicest temperament, and neither did any of us.

And from the sound of it, I don't think you have a nice temperament, either."

Thunder! Dragon come home, dirty-knot dog at the front door panting at his loafered heels, while the rest of us avoid him. Thunder! Dragon sits down, swallows the dining room table and chairs. Thunder! Dragon gets up, melts into an infant condensation of himself, lightning scorching each iris, the ultramarine garbage-patch, the slag dump marring the shore. Thunder! His firebolt face the atmospheric equivalent of a magazine loader; the rest of us cower instinctively, a home-grown version of the hard lockdown drill. Thunder! Dragon ka-booms, nine cracked tongues bang out of his body, a crowding that sounds like an air raid siren, shattering glass in the high-rise condos, storm petrels sobbing and blown off course, whirlwinds and sandstorms and lion-faced eagles tearing small herds of antelopes to shreds. Thunder! Dragon swoops in from the south, swerves in from the north, comes barreling in from the west and the east. Thunder! Dragon grows horns, racing up out of his temples and careening around his head. Thunder moon, hay moon, buck moon, blood moon, kicking the living daylights out of the small herd of antelopes knit together behind the living room couch. Thunder! Dragon grabs hold, hoarfrost and hot squall and mile-long tornado. Thunder! Dragon bites down, a disaster that stretches backward and rattles molecular chains, small herd of antelopes morphs into a pack of banes in a stunted grove, struggling to break the spell

How human the problem of tending a fire, building my ugly pile of sticks

while the finches eat fat in the rain. Even as you melt, tiny dragon,

your weight could pull this birdhouse apart, unchecked baggage a hungry ghost's art,

the part in the tale where the roof is blown clear off the pig.

I've propped it up on pins and needles, splinted the thing like a broken bone, spat wishes at it

as if it weren't wooden, called it music, called it language, called it home. There is nothing

that makes this nursery rhyme last but the oink-oink-oink of my hammer-hoof wrath

at the blacks of your keyboard spine. It's a conundrum done up in DNA lacing,

this face that's facing the mirror on the wall. I see you, dragon, owling back at me,

unspooling your drunkard fairytales, the damnedest of them all

Little dragon, don't you dream of trees, of setting your little pitchforks upon them

and scratching them til they bleed? Congress sweats in the Capitol gym

then grills the forests like franks on sticks at the bonfire for thinly veiled hatchet men

preening in their lumberjack drag, basking in the glow of a new Gilded Age,

while everyone at the party agrees the public weal is a dish that's best served cold and last.

By morning, nothing but tire tread, ecologists preaching to an assembly of stumps,

paw prints in the ashes where dragons lapped runoff, taking their dragon lumps in silence,

like parakeets during a storm. *The first song I heard was the warbling of a bird.*

The President lives in a lunch box leaking his meaty nibbles, repeatedly smaller bites of himself,

a thesis on the fractious snack in the jacked-up guts of "all the best people,"

an electorate dubbed the Mandelbrot set, government ads cocked and loaded, blam-blam-blamming

a quickfire ode to the clear-cutting à la mode behind a drive-through sandwich,

while feral finance chews cheese off the moon, stinking up the joint with its elevated musk

and little dragons watch quizzically, scratching their scaly heads. What led the Rüppell's griffon

to fly the friendly skies into the maw of the passenger jet was a love of thin air that hasn't quite yet,

despite our cockroach-in-cream machines, been beaten out of a vulture's dreams of a blue

that's the blue of the robes of an egg and a blue that's the blue of the seas' rolling eyes and a blue that's

the blue of the corn's lonely flower and a blue that's the blue of lightning and showers

and the blue of the morpho and the skipper's blue spots and the blue that's the blue of sorrow.

Up, up and away in my beautiful, my beautiful

The caged bird sits on her lathe-turned perch saying, "Fuck it, I'm not gonna sing"

In the scrim of the slim ribbon of green between the porch and the country byway,

an Eastern phoebe bobs its big head to and fro on a spindle-thin maple,

swallowtail, scattershot, stutters along. Even here, in this slender tea-sandwich strata,

this slice of spectral coordinates done up in mint, jade, juniper, parakeet, shamrock, emerald, moss,

in army and hunter and, wiser, in sage, in pine and pear and pickle, in olive and fern and chartreuse;

between a loose sort of home and a leaving, between the *graaaaaaaaahhh!* of a car's heated cardiology

and the heart that, looking, listens in; between the F-16 Viper Demo crashing in,

trashing the dum-da-dum finger-pad thrum of rain on leaves and the cardinal's bland counterpoint,

boxing the teenaged woods in the head with its flow-field decibel rock'em-sock'em,

shivering would-be timbers; between that and the soda can chucked out the window,

rattling onto the road's weedy edge; between the chest's fragile thumping and the milk-white air,

honeysuckle almost painfully fragrant, dragon crouched down in laneside scrabble, breathing a little,

rubbing his eyes, mourning dove oboeing prelude to vespers, chuck-will's-widow waking up;

abrupt as is the human engine explosion, the get-me-out-of-here heave-and-stroke,

underneath, inside, embedded within our spatula-slap eat-'em-up appetite for the next and the next

and the next place and thing, there's this singing. Dragon, do you hear it?

Prick up your pointy, synesthetic ears. It sounds green as cricket, tree frog, forest,

the feel of its ruffly, rapturous paws, the pheronome feast of the miniscule beasts tucked up under its

earthy pits. Dragon, this is it. This green is alive: 3425, 3435, 345, 355, 357.

Overwhelmed by its "lubb-dupp, lubb-dupp, lubb-dupp," we retreat into our usual pantone ways;

we've numbered heaven on earth. And, worse, we're counting down its days.

In our habitual, split-level, Cartesian haze, we can't see the forest for the lumber

Midday. Newshour. White-tailed skimmers loiter over the parking-lot potholes,

citrus thrips plunder the groves. Elsewhere the glittering demoiselle, elsewhere the humped knobtail,

the Cyprian plump bush-cricket clinging to rock-rose fingers, calling across the cow fields

to absolutely no one. Elsewhere the seedpod shieldback, elsewhere the fabulous green sphinx moth

battering the all-night furious lights at the world's largest missile base. Cloud copper, Vogel's blue,

Comoro friar. The two-spotted threadtail that lives in the rivulets where backhoes rumble and chew.

The Southern tailed birdwing, Madeiran brimstone, the Mesopotamian blue are flying feeding

fucking rubbing their fur-mat thighs on their wings, the allegro hum of airborne things,

the presto staccato glue that fuses the summer afternoon's smashed and shattered

and knee-bruise-gathered puzzlement back together, where wonder isn't canned like beans,

isn't shelled by executive privilege. Then poof. They disappear,

our commodity-crop chop-chop-chop an awful abracadabra, the planet sawed screaming in half.

Cameroon sparklewing, ancient greenling, Danish clouded Apollo

pinned to a map of a planet called Lost, while the citrus thrips suck at the lemon blossoms,

and the skimmers dump eggs in a pile of muck, trucks rattling by, caked with lovebugs

who adored the freeway atmosphere, the rank smell of diesel exhaust

House sparrows wrestle the chicken-bone litter, bathing ferociously in the tired dirt

beside the sad man pushing the mower. Push. Push. Push. Slow and ravishing,

ravishing and slow, the longest performance in musical history can't beat

euphonious trash-trees of sparrows, who've held their song three hundred times longer than we have;

pint-sized machines grubbing our crumbles, darning the tonal-atonal divide,

knitting their little livings into our infrastructure's insides, flexing their mobbed-up brutish force;

house sparrows chewing cigarette butts, bullying bluebirds with "whatchu want, tits?"

booting them from their boxes, yanking pigeons' drawers down and spanking their tufted asses,

feathers in house sparrows' scumbag caps; parking lot birds, ductwork birds,

little blow jobs that squat in tailpipes and the ribbed vents of household dryers, screwing in the lint;

sparrows that trip the grocery door and raid the hot bar and shit on the floor,

who've dealt with our crap since the Paleolithic and always come back for more—

Even their goose might be cooked. It was Mao Zedong who took command

of the people's banging of pots and pans, so the nerve-wracked sparrows couldn't land

and dropped like hail from the skies, and that was the start of the famine

when the bird-freed locusts ravaged the crops, and the people, too, fell like flies.

In Madrid, London, Philadelphia, Mumbai, the exhaust-fan bird, the lamppost bird,

the bird that fetched the souls of the ancient Nile's dead, that Chaucer called a lecher,

the bird of Psalms and Proverbs, the bird of Matthew and Luke,

with its junk-food, utility-pole, concrete style, shows signs of giving in,

a canary in a sparrow's suit, with a house sparrow's bib and its go-for-broke spin,

auguring the earth's rebuke, and meaner days on the horizon

Oh breath. (Breath.) The sky inside us, a dragon's dubious gift.

Amid a sack of fenced watches dumped on the bed, a dead-arm, sprung-lung

countdown to election where anyone can be President so somebody is, coughing

up an abyss. Dragon wheezing the breath of the pine trees, minted, billionaire-fresh,

wheezing the beery breath of the birch tree, the breath of the apple, worm-vexed and clawed,

breath of the white oak, the American beech, breath of the maple oozing sweet fraud,

breath of the mulberry losing its guts, breath of the gingko, slutty and tough,

Dragon wheezing, paler than pale; breath, pungent stuff of living, cuffed and roughed and jailed

The woodland is a simulacrum, stitches and stuffing staged behind glass

in the storefront museum off strip-mined Main Street, flesh scooped out and dumped in big boxes,

small-town America almost as gone as the glue-stick reeds and the bead-eyed, wire-framed foxes.

Vacuum-packed 12-piece of modified chicken comes boneless home to roost,

wrapped in plastic and bagged in plastic and wheeled to the family wagon,

13 high-performance plastics molded for seven buckled-in asses, stuffing our faces with poly-vinyls,

crumbs falling to floor, American red-white-and-more-more-more-more fluttering from the antenna,

radio tuned to the stink-gland brand of news that robs the hen house,

freedom a glovebox loaded with heat while driving to supper's fast-casual meat,

our legs' failed hookup with walking, the ghost in modernity's chronic bad mood.

It's a wonder a junco can hear itself trill over the power plant's edge-of-town cough,

and maybe we need a half a week off? TSA clipping Samsonite locks,

rifling spring break's spare set of socks like federally funded Delilahs,

pilgrims dragged bleeding from cheap seats, pilgrims ouching toward Babel,

as private jets ply the privatized sky, copyrighting cumulus clouds with their trademark contrails,

while elsewhere in the universe, nebulae preen in peacock green, supernovae glisten,

a faraway robot floats farther on, singing a wanderer's endless song about space, with no one to listen

All of us rotting on tenterhooks for the night when the moon passes out at the wheel,

skids into Earth's black-concrete shadow, and the earth drops its sober and follows along,

wrapping itself around 200 flag poles, swallowing its tail like a fistful of Adderall,

sparkling sparkling then flaming right out, a burn in the throat like demonic possession,

humanity's head boiling over and spinning like a top, cursing its feckless parents,

spitting up prop-room green pea soup, its little-girl limbs gone whack-a-doodle,

scratching company logos into its pancake-base face.

Such is the pace of our fabric's unravel. You think it will come in swatches and samples?

Guess again. It will be like fast fashion, petrochemical and ill of fit,

but so cheap-cheap and matchy-matchy that it's difficult to resist,

in the ultraviolet bug-zapper dusk, a final monumental *zzzzt*, and all of our wings collapsing,

space junkies jockeying in the petrified lanes of distant broken planets,

wads of useless currency, rubber band–muzzled like smuggled birds,

burning holes in their jumpsuit pockets, fevered as dying stars

Spiderweb bucks like a mule in a gust, kicks the morning sun to the dirt,

but spider, she cowgirls on, clutching the thing with one skinny-assed arm.

Spiral, ellipsis, circles in square. We think we invented geometry.

Silk so fine that hummingbirds, ruby-throated robbers, line their munchkin pockets

with web (and with lichen and dandelion down), silk so tough that the air flips its wig,

teasing strands from a spider's small hand and lifting her up as she fixes the cheesecake moon

in her sights, adoring it for its darkness as much as for its light. Spider takes flight,

ballooning over acephate lawns, over vacuum-sealed houses, central air on,

over the park, "an improvement upon nature," over the airport and its brand-name jets,

interiors as removed from the rapture of flight as interiors are able to get,

above the spindle-trunk second-growth timberlands and the 94 million cattle,

above the no-return horse-thieved wilderness dying in its saddle,

past the sand-castle coastlines where the kings hump the dunes

and the private-beach goon squad builds more and more rooms,

to the sea and its historical swells, its carracks and clippers and cogs and caravels,

past their spankers and staysails, their mizzens and jibs tense with wind,

bellied with the id of empire, a creeping deformation warping times hence,

to an island late-raised on a sea dragon's flare, and spiders are the only thing there

for history's hot minute, until the rockets' red glare of dominion blasts the feathers off the great auk,

its egg, akin to a toy top scribbled in child's ink, sold for 20,000 crowns, stalked

by all the museums, its flour-sack island sinking into a sea of brochure vacations,

beaches yummy as chicken. Or else to an island off a flim-flam bight where 600,000 fingers of light

grab the spider, fold over tight, as birds, exhausting their pocket-change might, fall all around her,

odds down the drain, spider caught in a human skein of mirrors and mixed emotions,

September's sad memorial cups filling up with terror, which is not, after all, our exclusive boast.

"The only good spider is a dead spider," says the arts administrator. "If I see a spider, it's toast."

The President steps onto the portico of this jerry-rigged year and squints into the retina sear

of the moon-stained sun, feigning a thermoset polymer of high molecular weight

molded into the shape of an idol of late hopped out of the reliquary and, Pinocchiolike,

come alive, the hate of the nascent millennium Geppettoing him into form, while a swarm

of ones and zeroes mistaken for birdsong and the buzzing of bees brings the congregation

to their knees, thinking him godlike before the eclipse; it's lie number 2,020,

though his blindness is genealogical. Well-awares on the fritz, the crowd wolfs him down

like he's Kibbles 'N Bits, paws up and begging in our dark paper spectacles,

some of us dying from making a living, some of us wearing manacles.

It's a long, slow crawl from here to the border in a pair of holey pants

on the trail of fears yanked out from under the desert's maniac plants,

where law and order dons its posh plumage and parrots the shoot-'em-up messaging in the wall:

I am the eye in the sky, looking at you, I can read your mind.

Cortez earned his bread and butter by turning the Aztecs to toast,

but we're in the infrared epoch now, the Rio Grande's heated coast a sacred calf,

its noggin smoked by radar like it's one big barbacoa. From Yuma, Arizona to Texas' Eagle Pass,

Homeland Security putt-a-putt-putts around on its ATV ass while a cheap dumpling angel

with a bellyful of gas jiggles like a cartoon float in the Macy's Day Parade, farting coordinates

over the radio to save America from a bushel of crop that's legal in Colorado,

the Chihuahuan Desert a mongrel panting in the continent's lap,

its hide bumpy with microchips, scratching and worrying its surgical scab

as a kestrel perches on the ripple-chip rust between La Patria es Primero and In God We Trust,

knowing a vole on either side tastes pretty much the same.

I can read your mind. I can read your mind

The operation before the operation? Drone strike. This is how our species communicates,

like black-clad Pilgrims devouring the centerpiece, plump-breasted, legs in the air.

Slide your feathers closer to the target, tiny dragon; see how the Pentagon spokesperson

resembles a hand puppet of Benjamin Franklin, wattles aflame, teasing out data,

a wing-dragging manipulation of a print-out that reads: *so happy together*

like a thundering gobble heard from afar, his forehead a gleaming Caucasian.

In the province of Marib, a car in which three men are riding is struck, prequel to

a disruptive medicine that the President calls "Thanksgiving" with a cluckety-cluckety-cluck.

A senior American official shrugs it off as a rare defect, a facial tick, a quantity of poults

hurrying, scurrying past the eye. "The sky is not falling," says the Army colonel,

burbling like a hunter who's swallowed his call. He looks like he doesn't quite know why

he's walking around with a stick in his mouth, a training tool, the wet hen hypothesis,

pricking the skittish airspace between feathers and an irresistible perch,

how Benjamin Franklin never, in fact, proposed the turkey as our national symbol.

Drones alighting, spreading their wings, soaring forward like eagles

Airspace? It's redundancy crumpling in on itself, crumpling and crumpling, crumpling crumpling,

a collapsible casket crammed full of feints, cratered with hoaxes turned horribly real.

The art of the deal between heaven and hell tucks into clam-shell gimcrackery and hurtles headlong

into the wall, an agenda composed of impact debris. On this what-now-woman morning

in this lock-her-up month in this go-back-to-where-you-came-from year,

fear wears a holster a billion guns long and strong-arms the 100-day make-nice

by cracking the shale reserves in the head, a gushing akin to anthropocide,

while out, far out, into the hole-punch cosmos, galaxies recede to avoid getting splattered.

What matters? College kids in the basement stockpiling birth control,

college kids in the basement stockpiling meds.

Down here in the basement, the worry is tectonic, while from up in the carbon-rich ether,

the crane leans down, far, far down, and smashes the earth in the face. They're constructing again,

on a Sunday, luxury condos with bespoke parking, cherried by green-washed roofs.

Ka-choong ka-ching, ka-choong, ka-ching, a heavy-metal strike-up-the-band

trumping the neighborhood's hallelujah, trumping the neighborhood's sleep.

This poem zipped up into full-metal jacket: *ka-ching ka-choong, ka-ching ka-choong.*

But ink is not just camouflage. When the big fish unveils its big banging teeth,

the octopus lets loose a ribbon of hormones that causes a predator to forget its greed.

It's wishful thinking, but the octopus might survive, while at the bottom of an oxygen-busted sea,

a robot lifts a tender finger, touches a long-lost world of shipwrecks, breathtakingly intact:

rudders, ropes, railings, and rigging, cargo hold encrusted in chains

Gone birding this late American morning, road closed on the margins of town,

tree removal or power lines down, battered Day-glo diamond sign: Sheriff's Inmate Crew Working.

Men, mostly brown and some of them white, in their wide, orange, jail-bird stripes, "afforded,"

as per the sheriff's website, an "opportunity" at "beautification," were picking trash off the road,

for which America, on average, has decided them owed 86 cents a day.

Three quarters, six pennies, a nickel, or eight dimes, a nickel, a cent. I went all the way

to the crane operator blocking the lane in his unionized seat, then turned around, and the sheriff,

wearing a who-are-you frown, pointed down the street. Take a right and a right and a right, he said,

toward the mud-cold lake striped by wind and patrolled by rough-necked swallows

What is above us? The trees, the trees. Or wasn't it once the trees, smeared with song

and the shitty behavior of birds, whose chatter is braggadocio for the pecking-order win-win-win,

or complaint, though it ain't a sin on this fruitless limb to weep, little dragon, for one's hungers.

It's springtime again, at least that was our plan, but the buds, tough nuts, refuse to break.

They won't spill the seeds on how trees roll up sleeves and reach out undercover,

the forest's secret embrace lingering in the dirt while the peat bog burns,

turning the trees' oxygen sighs into wheezing smog, a dragon's-breath cog in the human machine

that's churned the planet like I Can't Believe It's Not Butter!® as a blood-purple, beauty-vlog jerkbot

smirk does the work of selling the last leg of Bornean jungle down river,

where a great ape awakens from a crack to the skull amid the dull unfamiliar of stumps and soot,

and having to use a foot as a foot, knuckles onto the bird-ghosted road, a refugee seeking a home

Good-bye, Big Dipper; good-bye, Pleiades; goodbye, Orion, good-bye.

Underneath this dome leeching its incandescence into the sky,

the "what's that? what's that? what's that, what's that?" of the modern trade in attention disorder, our

faces booked, tried, and sentenced to life on a jag in a backlit hole,

snorting crystal liquid light, popping hot little privatized pixels,

Karl Marx in the airport terminal, pulling a wheelie cart, bowing his head,

cellular manifesto chirp-chirp-chirping in his sweating palm.

The citizenry, its stockings on, puts up its feet up, playing at dead,

as harmonic overtones ring from the sparrows nesting in the fluorescence overhead.

In the thumpalong cellophane-sandwich day, headaches and missed flights

and penance paid in backscatter X-ray and millimeter waves,

the tug of a black hole eating its heart out seven light years away

Look! Up in the sky, it's Space Force, a mission sincere as an air kiss

blown by a stunt man to the faint-hearted stars of a sci-fi western set upon Mars,

an intergalactic how-de-do in a deadly game of laser tag at the O.K. Corral on the final frontier,

a sermon called "Jesus: The Original Superman" with a Hollywood ending and a pair of tight buns,

sex bought and sold on tumbleweed planets, "a sort of desolate freedom," says the astronaut,

waxing his something poetic; Space Force, snagging the skin off the moon, ripping like barbed wire,

weed sprays and super seeds and beer-in-hand rovers branding the bushes on Venus and Neptune,

stars aligned for gain through ruin, the Milky Way a cow fattened on extraterrestrial grain.

It's Space Force demanding quasars bend over to cavity search their massive black holes,

Earth's high-net souls sucking up futures on astral metals like they're hoovering lines of blow,

their interstellar leisure yachts docked at outer space offshore havens on a sea we call emptiness,

while the silence, the great big silence around us, isn't, in fact, silent at all, just bribed to keep quiet

A flock batters in, the nineteen shadow selves of this poem clatter the polarized glass,

sheening it with brick-brown slurry, an avian darkness, each puny heart

a puny transistor of what might have been, while a bird, a real bird, just one bird,

eeps in the forest past the screened-in porch where my screened-in torch encases a sky

scattered with flutelike, cloudlike bones—airstream bones, languageless bones,

bones like an empty reliquary, bones like a spell gone "poof,"

rattling bones battling weekender drones, the red-tailed hawk versus the hobbyists

playing a game called kill-chain, our era's update of a reenactment of the Battle of Bushy Run,

Western Pennsylvania: American goldfinch, American redstart, American bittern, American crow,

nationhood tacking wings of things to a corkboard labeled "Native,"

the Battle of the Clouds a soggy suburban prelude to the Big Runaway,

the War of Independence a ploy for control of the meaning in "Native,"

my state replanted in musket balls, seeds of a leaden origin myth got up in cottony fluff:

a robin for good news, an owl for bad news, a bat for life and death,

the Kinzua Dam shoving its fist deep down the throat of the Allegheny,

flooding the Seneca Nation to keep Pennsylvania afloat

Icy conditions coming on, half the neighborhood up and gone,

cops roam the streets in the white out, guns drawn,

and this is not the weather report, though it does describe the climate,

cold burn forcing residents in or out of the pale dream: mowed lawns and American flags,

or the stars brought down and shackled to an x'ed-out era's undying, up a pole and flying

on either side of the line. Pennsylvania, where are you? State of my birth, re-mapping the past

on your upcountry paths, yanking southern latitude like waders over your northern knees,

your come-and-take-it tease flapping in the frostbite breeze, weekenders shitting bullets.

We say bullets fly. But they don't have wings. They're alloyed, propulsive, kinetic things,

spiraling to stay on course, tapered in order to bore; their supersonic center of force

unconstrained human intent taken as a matter of course, spent cartridge dropped to the floor.

What more can we want from America than a casual afternoon open carry for every

fidgety Tom, Dick, and Harry? Condor alights on the hunting grounds, scavenges lead-tainted kill

Confederate flags in Pennsylvania an aggressive version of the edge effect,

kingfishers tsking their irked asses off on the mud-pie banks of the Susquehanna,

effluvia dancing downstream; clouds all coursing in at once over the Endless Mountains,

endless freight depot a gash in their flank stitched up with cargo containers,

neon-trimmed dragonlike fracking well rising and rumbling, a rollercoaster trademarked Shale Play,

sylvan setting strapped in and careening agog downhill, dairy cows in the foreground

putting up their own special stink, all of us drinking the water still, all of us breathing the air.

Redmond 5H: "failure to properly control or dispose of industrial or residual waste"

Smurkowski S Wyo 5H: "failure to take all necessary measures to prevent a spill"

Hope 1H: "failure to plug an abandoned well." Something is rotten in the Commonwealth,

no wonder they call it Marcellus, weeping slab of hardened mud hammered by kings and spectres,

slippery benzene bobby pins picking the rocks' 19,000 locks, raiding the Middle Devonian coffers,

methane leaking like White House dirt all over the contract-dazed neighbors. "It's a neat pair,"

says the industry hack, pawing a pert set of federal treats, reaping the smutty benefits.

Like Silly Putty in child-sized hands, we stand for god and country,

and suck the bejesus out of this land like we're tonguing a piece of hard candy,

a handy metaphor for our impossibly bottomless hunger,

Pennsylvania's gullet jammed open and force-fed unsavory nuggets:

biocides, breakers, friction reducers, oxygen scavengers, sand—

$70 billion of beach dredged out from under a goose's webbed feet, along with all the water,

goose left standing on a slab of concrete, pipeline spitting gas beneath streets

to the golf club kitchen to fuel the heat on our order of seared foie gras

Freshly dipped, the President glows the offshore glow of oil rigs and wobbly tankers,

the glow, with thanks to bankers, of bombs burst in air, the glow of continual authorized force,

a Trojan horse with 1,000 dark bellies and one contemptible trick, to stick 'em up again

and again, a scalable, portable, modular mechanics of mugging in the American interest,

the security state a clusterfuck, a secret humping a secret humping a secret humping a secret,

while at the Maneuver Center of Excellence for the Firearms and Tactics Division,

a FedBizOpps for a set design of a half-eaten breakfast and a child's toy left in the yard,

Fort Benning done up in urban street drag, ICE caught holding the hyper-realistic bag

for "the replication of battlefield conditions," if the battle were in Chicago or Tucson.

Oh, geese, who trust air to bear you, with your adenoids and your chinstrap face on,

as you cup your wings and gently skate onto the phosphorus gunk of this lake,

in this park in this town in this state in this god-forsaken union, geese: What have we done?

The President lies in a vacuum where the President doesn't exist, scratching the itchy sutures
where his fun strings are attached. Hatched from their opportunist eggs, the courtiers
scratch right back, flipping their powdery louse-eaten lids, farting explosive laughing gas
at the President's dull load of filler, inside where a ticking bomb makes no sound,
inside where all the rotten melons fall apart without stinking, inside amid the fashion
in oxygenated party tricks, inside a positively Medieval beau monde, where auto-da-fé
is the plat du jour, dabblers chronically throttling themselves to prove they were formerly breathing.
Inside the methane-plume nursery, President Baby melts right down, straps the little plastic people
into a tiny muscle car, hurls it across the room. Frowning at the terrarium, dashing it off the shelf,
President Baby tickles himself, he giggles and giggles and giggles, while outside
a worm-eating warbler fidgets, outside an indigo bunting sings his bluer-than-bluer-than-blues

Common yellowthroat, red-eyed vireo, scarlet tanager, bay-breasted warbler;

termites hatching in Brooklyn today, and a weary bird's gotta eat.

Dragon, tuck your napkin in, it's a tiny, noisy dinosaur feast;

their least concern this uproarious dawn is our desperate grab at oblivion:

black-throated blue pill, black-crowned night pill, ruby-crowned king pill, cerulean pill,

a flock of capsules and tablets and caplets to wing us into a stinging smoglike simulation of sleep,

boutique swaddlers paid to pack us in ticks-n-tocks, in rocking boxes, pharmacological portmanteaus

shipped overnight from workaday one to workaday two to workadays three, four, and five,

lenticular clouds in the cubicles, stars in the tech team's pillowcase eyes

pulling all-nighters at the $10 million startup pushing a branded misspelling of "dream,"

analysts betting unconsciousness is as lucrative as hacking your genes

for a woke of vampiric dimensions, the disruption of the mean inconvenience of years,

savants of the Valley of Heart's Delight drenched in nanotechnical tears, frozen in fear of dying,

while a broken-bone crow who's known her own woes looks up, asks the sky for its witness

Scrape. As if the sky were a knee and the cloud cover Band-Aids, quilted plastic, lawyerly and elastic,

between heaven and the bare-naked plovers, between heaven and the gobsmacked gulls.

How teeny-tiny the labyrinth beneath us, cosmetic enrichment by way of remove:

lobbyists goose step in sugary boots, fanning their tails on the avenues like Mummers,

while networks swap bummers for spangled parades, the newsroom an ag-gagged clucker.

Up here, the architecture fluffs its pucker, unfurls its fairytale trusses to the copters

and flocks of plastic bags, the hags on their analog broomsticks wheeling

wheeling wheeling and wheeling, punch-drunk on diodic light. Is it right to

cut the troposphere's throat with a razor the heft of a pod of blue whales?

Whosoever fails at the breakthrough listen—the glistening dream of the clerk of the storms,

the woozy tether at the end of Earth's arms—can beanstalk their way to eternity here,

at $11,000 a square foot, head a-slosh with ballast, the palace flip-flopping an inch at a time,

a rhyme in classical iambs, an apt evocation of wind on cliffs, minutes of blessed weightlessness,

as below, the rigs swoon with over-production, a pot-sick scrabble suggesting Hephaestus,

while every so often, the chorus steps forward, sweeps a slick-dashed pelican up in its arms

Would you mind now, shivering dragon, if I leave you like my mother's mother

dispatched a roasted hen, sucking the fat from her fingernails, chewing the bones,

and then mashing its liver, frying its gizzard, boiling its heart and neck?

Oh, let me alone, little dragon, bank your turn and forget;

it's a laugh when you know you're drawing The Tower before you've shuffled the deck.

The stars don tits and wigs tonight, shake asses down the runway of the legendary sky,

and tiny dragons drag themselves off the lawn, unwrinkle their wings, flex middle fingers, and fly.

They're gone where the corn clenches its teeth and whirls silken ears toward the clattering sky,

while the farmer turns a blind eye to this a priori knock-down of the problem of the beetle

and drowns the place in poison, a government gift that threads the needle

for the fumigatory titans of industry, whose code name means "my saint."

Swooping in on the agencies and ravaging acres of ethics agreements,

the visitor logs prone to a plague of winged redactions, it's snack time in all its gory release,

the takeout-salad tables of the oversight committees groaning beneath the deregulated feast,

meeting room seats swiveled so fast, it's enough to give a bureaucrat whiplash,

gods of the federal benefits package willing. Dragon, let's break for a story:

In 1890 Henry Davis Minot, son of Northeastern cotton-wad riches, met his end

in a train wreck because the railroads were bitches that he himself had unleashed,

their canines gnashing the continent's spine from Boston to Alki Beach.

As a younger man, he had romanced the avian, studious and ornithologic.

But it wasn't avarice that had him run for those shady hills of profit.

It was that Hank had a nervous breakdown, as if his five pound guide to New England birds

was flung from the height of a carrier pigeon, spanking him in the head.

Some people just can't abide by the fact that we have always been nature's instead.

Instead of clear-cutting, forests. Instead of strip mining, mountains.

Instead of climate change, islands where the dodo bird once lived. Or, instead,

there's a time-share condo on the beach, the reach of an alclad aluminum wing as great as the yolk-wigged gannet, who falling in love with a hand-painted replica of his kind,

nests on the cliff wall's behind, grooming a bird-shaped block of cement, all with the rangers'

well-meaning intent to trick the instead out of the stout, red heart of a seafaring bird.

Nature's a blunt but oft-ignored teacher struggling for attention from our unruly class,

while we take life on Earth for a well-curved quiz that we can get mostly wrong and still pass.

Today, the suet I hung beneath the mildewed roof of the feeder whose walls are rotten

swings on its chain forgotten. And shaken by the absence of the woodpecker,

his warning-sign head atop prison-stripe shoulders, I smolder a bit with desire to fix this line

that's hanging here, find the right word that summons the bird,

like islanders missing their gannets. They called him Nigel, or dammit,

they called him No Mates, instead. And he died there, his love refused.

When he reached for her feathers to preen her cold shoulders, that block of cement couldn't coo

"It's image salad," says the yellow-billed cuckoo. Fair enough. Let's check in on the Agencies:

Department of State? Obedient walrus. Pats its head and rubs its belly,

balances a globe on its fishy nose, buttering up the popcorn crowd of Arctic explorers

sweating in their fancy pants, perspiring all over Finland, Finland politely ahem'ing.

It's 84 degrees Fahrenheit at 64 degrees north, and the Interior Secretary is yawning,

"I haven't lost any sleep over it." He's snuggling into his slippery sheets

with their 415 ppm thread count, the midnight toads' bassooning,

the sexed-up mosquitos' falsetto lulling him into a carbon dioxide fantasia,

where Anne Sexton in her white fur coat guns the engine in modernity's garage,

hands him a vodka martini. Fuming over a panda cam focused on nothing but nothing at all,

the President issues a trigger warning: "They could cut a hole in it, dig under it, climb over it,"

his goosebumps pornographic, while the EPA feigns an asthma attack and ducks out of Algebra II.

It's an ace in the hole on a golf course in Greenland, a serpent coiled in a bluebird box.

"It's gold and diamonds and fishes galore, a new arena for competition, new opportunities,

new threats, a new age of strategic engagement. It's real estate!" gargles Department of State,

salivating all over the bit in his mouth. Treasury stuffs his skinny arms through the loopholes

in the kiddie floats, jack-knifes into the crypto-currents of the continent's waterlogged flood maps,

clutching an invitation to a heated pool party where the guest list is confirmed as a matter of rote,

and fuck all conflicts of interest. Bureau of Land Management, going in for the kill,

stalks a couple of underaged hikers, flings them into a coal seam in the bingo-hall hills of Wyoming,

and the President fluffs his pompoms with a "Push 'em back, shove 'em back, way back!"

Science collapses in a heap on the field. It's the history of chlorpyrifos plagiarized

by an influencer with a toxic thumbprint and a handle swiped from a nightclub

masquerading as the mystery in a packet of seeds, a moon-pie meditation with a 401K

piled atop the neighborhood's neck-snapping reversals, like we're standing under a falling tree,

which is falling falling for a long long time, falling all the goddamned way down,

the last falling tree in the universe, and nobody acknowledges the sound

A cardboard cutout sex doll plays pattycake with the far-gone right at the face surveillance fan con,

its error margin inflation unleashing a flood of fresh-cracked converts because

nobody likes a mistaken identity more than a party of handgun enthusiasts weary of paper targets.

The taffy governor yanked from his chair and wrapped around 300,000 itchy trigger fingers

standing their glyphosate ground, a 653 million-square-mile slab of blubber in the shape of Florida.

White-eyed parakeet, white-crowned pigeon, white ibis, white-winged dove,

white guy pops a Glock at the Quik Mart because parking is a matter of soil and blood.

Not birds in cages but babies in cages, the icy new rule of the land. "Mom, I wanted

to remember your face," says the child officially kidnapped at a checkpoint on the Rio Grande,

"I was so afraid of forgetting what you looked like. I wanted to remember your face."

Gravity claims the giant haystack nest of the present,

a weaving of wires and the will to be watched

collapsing down to the size of the bleeping skunk in one's pocket;

technology, laying thin-shelled eggs, gives birth to a zillion gaping eyes,

a boundless brood of business interests, beaks wide open for the integrated kill,

a jackalope called American appetite, born of a massive marketing budget

humping an infrared camera trap. Coincidence flown the coop

along with the passenger pigeons, the skies turned grey with predator satiation,

a robotic iteration of 850,000 bored grandpas, farting on sidewalk milk crates, spying on neighbors,

the digital age rendering even stool pigeons obsolete. Radio-frequency energy

an electronic version of guano, there's shit—the meme—all over our heads.

It's a post-accountability kingdom in which everyone is accounted for 40 million times a day.

In the romance of fingerprint recognition, microchip drilled under the skin hiccups

whenever an employee sins, a bathroom-stall selfie gone soft, as the President in his bouncy castle

bounces bounces bounces, shouting, "Say 'cheese,' say 'cheese,' say 'cheese!'"

The President's favorite recipe for the President's slice of the whole condemned pie:

Take the cricket out of the bluebird's mouth, pull the bluebird down from the sky,

drain the sky of its cyan and indigo, its sapphire, azure, cobalt, and teal,

steal the owl from the trees' embrace, erase the tree and the forest that hugs it,

tug the reeds from the blackbird's feet, drain the blackbird's sweetgrass swamp,

chomp the brush and flush the snipes, wipe the soil clean of its blossoms,

and throw away all the bugs. Pull the rug from under the buzzard's fine breeze,

squeeze the lake dry and evict all the grebes, plug the yawning holes with sprawl.

On this leftover tinpot fragment of dirt orbiting a burning hurt, now you can build your wall

The puffy blue glove of morning lies on the sidewalkless Midwestern street, and no, it's not

a fragment of sky; it's a petroleum product digitized, insulation against the prairie's white frost,

less its lesser chickens, plucked clean of its native grass, the Great Plains bald as an baby's ass,

and lonesome something awful, while up above us, clashing traumas clang, clang, clang,

the siren that used to forewarn us of storms suppressed by bright, new technologies,

the menace before the freak-out a nostalgia for analogue anger,

squall-eyed god mouths cracking with thunder, hammers hurled from miles above,

driving studs clear through the universe to the acid-peel other side, where time looks

like a plywood floor buckling beneath a fat load of fear that's called Where Are They?

Where are the claw heads, where are the pliers, where are the scalpels and sutures and stanches?

Where are the tool-belt saviors? Why don't they yank out the booby traps embedded in our skin?

We are fastened here to the hydraulic-gun epoch; its pop!-pop!-pop!-pop! turns us inside out,

our faces beds of bleeding nails, stumbling forward, banging our heads. Can I trouble you

for a saw and bow? Twang a sad old cattle-prod tune; like the prairie chickens, we'll dance

To the air, the air! That carries everything on it: balm, breath, mist, melody, Medieval philosophy,

rough-n-tough radio, static with the hate that broadcasts things we need to know about humans,

ourselves, humans, our logics unmoored and soaring out over the fields of alfalfa,

hackberry, nettle, wild licorice, mallow and clover and mustard, that sunstroke plant

whose coincident scent is scant reason to force it to wed, if in name alone, a weapon

so chemical that it burns the air drawn down into the body's fleecy pockets, a blinding embrace

that races through bone to bore its way into the future. We suture nature to our illest intent,

poem begun in a lump sum of sun, rent from its flight and torpedoing the rampartless village

with prime-time applause for symbolism's dependent clause and the pillage at the end of the line.

Fine. To the air, then, to a step and a salt and a reel, to graces and the feel of the thousand ugly faces

we make in a day of wagery, kicking our greasy balls of debt down and down the years, slipping

and tripping over ghosts of past purchase, clubbed up like divots of sod, while the dirigible class

tosses pellets to the mob, peers through opera glasses from its philanthropic cloister,

slurping the soft-bodied tax codes up, the goddamned world its oyster. To the air, friends,

ushering hypersonic missiles into the theater of insects to blitz aisles of blooms; to the air

making its naked dash from the wings, tearing the curtains asunder, streaking across the stage,

the bare-naked air, the undressed air, unabashedly bending and blowing itself, the filthy-dirty air,

dropping its drawers on the planet's glib floors, birthday suiting the spoiler alert,

hopping out of the cake: "Surprise! It's me! The air!" which is also only a medium,

above the surface the one and only we've got. Let's stop being afraid to fill up our chests,

and to let our chests deflate. Must we poke and prod and berate tiny dragons,

dissect them into formaldehyde pieces to prove that they dream of the air?

Between the clocking you took at your birth, tiny dragon, a spit-shine, indigo, hard-pressed clank

that's engined this Earth as it cranks off the cliff, and the clocking you handed down in balled fists,

between our bruises and the President's ticking gold bomb, between the President,

any President, and the dawn of humankind, when a blind fish wobbled up an oversteep slope

with the hope of a cosmic resilience, there's been a microtone, a minim, a modicum of time

jammed with the glissando crescendoing chime of a species' mass beaching in the universe,

like pilot whales fleeing from sharks, but worse, for we're taking the sharks with us also.

It is dark now in the chemicalized citizenry's head, in our smog-blanket Jupiter-tempest bed,

as the Reaper drones lift from the desert, a tensile imperial flock. On Michoacán's central peaks,

winter's butterfly hugs the oyamel firs where tailings of copper mines line the mud streets;

then a butterfly two generations hence, tottering along on rag-tag wing,

flutters through fenced autumns and springs into North American fields slam-dunked in neonics.

Is there no goddamned thing that we haven't forced upon it? It's a blessing, the butterfly

that lands on your dress, not because it is anything with a meaning but itself.

As a billion American travelers like me recline to our seat-belt window-side views

with our soggy, carry-on lunches and our downloaded airplane-mode news

over Florida, a smudge, a boggy erasure, south across the border, an arrant enclosure,

chasing butterflies back to their touristic haunt, it's butterflies butterflies butterflies we want

to pose for our ravenous cameras. The stamina it takes for a butterfly, or a child,

to weather a punishing 3,000 miles to make it to here from there or further,

expecting, if not our care, then not torture at our hands, stands as the continent's greatest test

of if we're blessed or cursed at all, benediction being the writing on the wall we are willing to read

in this age of anger over elemental needs and our anti-grieving nostrums

The President speaks, and it's a landfill emission, it's a mega-drill fracturing shale.

The President speaks. It's an oil well blowout, it's a seismic air gun silencing

the woop-woop music of whales. The President speaks. It's lead ammunition,

it's dry-cleaner solvent, it's toxic copper filter cake. The President speaks; it's billowing coal dust.

It's a train hauling flammable liquids straight through the NIMBY front gate.

While the President eats his endangered dinner, while he cranks up his jack-in-the-box, let us

climb to the top of the President's tower, ride its glittering lift like it's a beautiful woman's cock.

We'll take stock of the world from this creaky zenith, plant our bare asses on its ledge and unlock

a whopping view: pinking clouds and the sun humming its sonorous setting song

over a river filling with sandhill cranes, the great wet roost purring like a bed of overfed cats,

the marsh awash in wingbeat with the going of geese and the coming of blackbirds by the millions

upon millions upon millions, then Venus, Saturn, Jupiter, Mars, the full-bellied moon,

and us here, my loves, tits out and lightning bolts dripping,

singing our cataclysmic tune, a monsoon of response to the migrating flocks,

a pox on the President's particulate matter, the filth at the end of his pen.

When dragon uncurls on night's shimmering bed, meteors streaming from his trapezoid head,

you know Earth is ploughing through deep shit. The President doesn't give a wit.

Sandwiched in his mirrored den, the President, ad nauseum, sees President President President,

Stockholm syndrome rebranded as an echo chamber for one. We're done with this leveling age of

improvement, the movement of sound waves from bellowing rockets ripping through rainbows,

tearing new assholes out of the sky, flame-throwing lies burning through nations

like a mega-fire on a dry-hump jag, California in the bag and popping like microwaved popcorn.

"It was so loud," says the evacuee, "you could hear the trees exploding. Pow, pow, pow!"

We are up here with the chimney swifts now, and like them, we don't need perches;

as the President lurches from a vista of the back of his head to a vista of his face,

we stand and arch and flip off into space, navigating by sight and scent,

by the planet's infrasonic rant, by the bloody delicious stars, out above the President's tower,

which is made of mud, which lists and leans and lurches, then topples with a thud

You don't guard a flaming pearl, tiny dragon, you don't guard a golden fleece,

you're not the kind of dragon for sword fights and safekeep; with your thirst like a camel,

your hunger like hogs, you land in a smog of disasters and *cut the clouds full fast*

but I have gorged, tiny dragon, on the pillage you've amassed, some of it rotten, some of it sweet,

your drunk eyes as red as winter's stored apples, your drunk eyes as red as summer's raw meat,

you fucked with the weather, turned off the moon, tattooed your image on my back with your teeth,

and always I feel followed. In these duck-blind poems I hide inside, loaded and pointed and cocked,

what's to stop me from going ballistic? There is nothing to cease the lockjaw grinding,

send the monkey packing in his combustible pillbox hat; I've been hacking up fire,

hot and cold and dry and wet, a net of sweat and cluster bombs, since the universe was in diapers, and

still, I could forget every open-sesame, every secret word to herd the turbulent, flesh-eating bird off of

my chest where it shits on my thoughts and devours the rest of the chorus,

a burn like the runaway greenhouse effect that turned Venus to porous junk,

a lump of boiling porridge even Goldilocks would reject. Where, in such appetite, can grace be met?

Let's direct the story toward the bears' grief in finding their sense of place made brief

by human business. Sadness is their witness. The sadness of a map of the world as big as the world and

equally torn. We are born to such a chart as this; I can GPS my birth in its tatters,

and all that matters is to find a route through each angry shred, to see sadness ahead

in the middle of the lane, a ball of hunger, ticks, and mange, and to stop there

and quietly watch while it passes. Tiny dragon, how staggering it feels,

my engine idle, breathing for real, world come alive in your ashes

The hardball of the car alarm ricochets off the city walls, and cracks the teensy teacup ear

of the swallow, who, chirping, stops chirping to compose a considered response, while we wallow

in our caution-tape wherefores, oblivious to the exchange. Rough beasts, you and I,

lumps of clay erupting, tiny volcanoes melting the streetscape as we hurry along on our

wham-bam way. Here is the trigger and here is the blast, here is the hunk of metal

in the fleshed-over wound, a "fuck" in your head, fuzz on the tongue, your pupils differential,

an emergency interruption in the otherwise bland and businesslike day,

like the whole damned world missed the sound check, dragon, and now

your ears are filled with blood, muffling the ice breakers' clanging upriver

and the fog horn's oh-no-no-no-no. What do dragons suggest?

Bad weather and plenty of it, rain come down like bullets, and bullets come down like rain.

Dragon, your claws are made of blown glass; when you dance us across the living room rug wearing us

on your feet, the weight of family shatters them and scatters them like shrapnel.

With the living room rug as my witness, and the swallow that's socked by our hullabaloo,

and the pink flamingo as witness, too—a father of eight, a survivor of floods, who lay in the mud

of a Balkan zoo while boys barely ready for two-plus-two kicked him until he was finished—I pray

a dragon's wings, hard as rusks, soften in the milky dusk and melt themselves into an updraft.

May your talons, in glassy glitter and shards, constellating like hot little stars, strafe the night

with their razzamatazz, pulse like beacons from a billion-mile distance, and everyone feel safe

Whether they were jonesing for heaven or thought it just a fable, I'm unable to have known, but

all day people came to me to speak about the souls bundled in feather and empty-pocket bone:

the tall, thin dad clad in a heron's cold blue steel, stock-still and staring, then peeling off the lake;

someone's mother in the honeysuckle, chasing down its nectar on a sugar-water high,

another as the stoplight-bellied hectorer of spring. And you, tiny dragon, a scaly-assed, four-winged,

prickle-tooth thing, hiccuping a drunkard's firewater sputter, the finches muttering

and inching down the perch, here's a chance for the attention you craved, and why not?

Why not you, the afterlife's most improbable agent, passing for a vagrant in a pastoral scene?

Now the neotropic flock, by the lights of a hand-me-down planetary clock,

braves the wide and queasy Gulf, its sleazy drilling platforms and its fee-fi-fo-fum rummaging for oil,

from its spoiled southern jungle to its spoiled northern coast flush with cell towers

made to look like ugly trees. These souls, who've been arriving before places were our places,

we've erased them as they are, and in the super-duper blue of the bunting,

in the graphite-pencil grey of the wren, we've penned them into being, not birds, nevermore,

but versions of ourselves. We all need a way to remember the dead,

but dragon, let us shelve these mystical urgings. I don't know what you are,

though you made me what I am. By the light of the sun and the exasperated stars,

by the yank of the earth and its flabbergasting smells, chart your flight path by yourself.

Go ahead and scram. I don't believe in heaven, but I'm not sending you to hell

In the woods this morning, the chipmunks' complaint, which I don't want to liken to squeaky toys,

having sought myself free of the price-tag noise of department-store shelvesful of manufacture;

then up with the hemlocks on the pillowcase slope, where chipmunks, preferring deciduous clutter,

didn't utter a peep, I got the dope from the corvids in the distance: yack-yack. Then back

down the steep incline to the car, where I didn't get far before the rodents were screaming

because you can't win for losing with chipmunks. It is true that often I drive to my poems,

or at least to the heads of their trails; I fail everyday at being bigger than human, and tinier too,

but, dragon, I'm exhausted with framing you for my flaws. Let the law abolish its perp walks;

in this forest of disappearing blazes, I've looked for the path that leads from the spot where hurt talks

louder than healing to the spot where there's no talk at all, no checklists, no field guides, no naming,

everything just what it is. Dying: It was a small performance, your gnarly scales, legendary scales,

smoothing into a sort of pudding, a creamy pearlescent pudding of face,

a coastal fog face, precipitous, a blur; with my theriophobic fear of your beast,

I witnessed your melting from an arm's arm's length; spatula in hand,

I could have spread you like lard in the megafaunal medical glare, tiny dragon,

so there; it's not hard to imagine you grey-green ash stashed in a box in a drawer in a wall

with all the rest of the war-hero dead, though sometimes still you batter my head

like a meadowhawk fastened to light. Dying didn't solve the problem of yourself;

tiny dragon, you're still on the hook. But I'm not one to leave you there, rotten, uncooked.

Like the warbler I watched pluck the glassy wings from the meadowhawk's armored thorax,

I've digested each soft, collateral clue of my baffling, filial need for you

so I could earn the nerve to move on

I have seen gulls harass an osprey on the cold California coast, seen an osprey harass an eagle

on a finger of lake in New York, watched black-capped chickadees storm Nebraska's winter feeders,

heard buntings and tanagers bellow from the Appalachian scruff, awoke to cedar waxwings

owning the clapboard side streets of Maine, and boat-tailed grackles, those shimmering roughs,

heard vireos practice their nursery rhymes, watched Western bluebirds fuck,

followed kettles of broad-shouldered hawks riding the thermals, corkscrewing south,

I have conjured you, tiny dragon, with the egret in the garbagey reeds shoving fish in its mouth,

with the worm-eating warblers at Bad Creek, and the mocking birds blabbing at Table Rock,

with the Rio Grande's curve-billed thrasher and the Rio Grande's collared dove

and the swallows of San Francisco in the mercury-weighted fog, I have nested you here

in the sand dunes amid the husks of washed-up traps, hatched you from a blotchy egg,

taught you a yolky flight, belched grubs down your throat, tore dew-nets to shreds,

chewed the metal bands off your ankles. I have conjured you, miniscule dragon, as small

as small can be, I have conjured you, little monster, so that you'd fledge and set us both free

Bee: the beginning of names, the drone before drones, the thing that means hover,

means vibrate, means rouse, the ferocious task of staying aloft, the ferocious task of enduring;

not the chair falling out from under the seated, bruises blooming on ass;

not the takedown of low-rise buildings, wrecking ball smack-smack-smacking the brick,

their Icarian replacements in bitcoin and glass;

not the give-way of rusty-gut byways, with a near-biological loosening of belt;

not the bone-felt fray of the safety net, the Cabinet, real cutups, unhinging their shivs,

the President pushing his pop-up book trilogy: *Who Loses?*, *Who Wins?*, *Who Lives?*

Not the rollback of the anti-corruption rule, rollback of the anti-mine waste rule, rollback of the anti-

pesticide rule, rollback of the ozone pollution rule, rollback of the arsenic dumping rule, rollback of

the rule against greenhouse gas, against pipelines, against drilling the coasts,

not the rollback of the Clean Air Act, citizens hacking into their sleeves, enjoying the great indoors;

not everything bloodlet by tiger mosquitoes, everything smothered in kudzu.

Not icebergs sweating like animals, birthing catastrophic calves, mooing and menacing Greenland.

Not baobab trees fallen to their knees, begging the skies for a goddamned drink.

"This is a sad story," says the scientist, as a kangaroo hurtles through the living room window,

punches the daylights out of the post-pastoral decor, falls to bits on the powder room floor,

weeping for its outback. Not a heap of cracked spines and packing tape,

a monument to the fallen fulfillment center worker entitled *Un Bien Ruïné*,

the richest man in kingdom come, with a name he stole from the ancient embattled daughters,

coughing up compensation in so many Styrofoam peanuts, like he's force-feeding baby warblers.

Not far too few warblers, not far too few whooping cranes, not far too few Molokai creepers,

pistol popping across the road at 6 pm on a Tuesday evening in August, and not collapse.

Not sew-bots, not algae blooms, not forced-labor chicken tenders.

Not collapse. On this bullfrog-song, cricket-hum evening in the absentee hills of PA,

Eastern bluebird, Eastern phoebe, Eastern meadowlark pipe right down,

tucking a beak and a crooked knee, and propping one pooling eye open because the world just isn't safe enough to rock the head's whole nest to sleep—

nest of grass and plastic trash, library stacks and uncontrolled burning,

an economist's cotton-mouthed yearning for a forest knocked on its wooden keister,

the dawn chorus downsized to digital hold music programmed by outsourced thumbs,

so when the morning comes, headphones and pink slips; economists, quaint in their hard hats,

with clipboards and No. 2 pencils, chirping, "check, check, check, check, check, check, check."

The orangutan versus the bulldozer, a slippery revision entitled *Are You My Mother? 2.0*,

the murder in packaged snacks. Not that, but the bees:

masons, carpenters, wool carders, diggers, builders of honied hives,

sentries and lovers and killers and queens, pollen gooping their thighs,

cosmological gatherers counting backwards to zero, to the universal egg.

"I certainly wouldn't use the word 'consciousness,'" says the professor of psychophysics,

bees bumbling his head. Foragers cha-cha-cha-ing to the music of thrumming stars,

tasting the air with their suction-cup feet; hives, the galaxy's honkytonk bars,

silly with sex and sweet emotion, hairy chests donning boutonnières of a million million blossoms,

sunlight dripping from combs. Don't just slump there on your barstool,

tiny dragon, let the raucous bees carry you home

Go, little dragon, go and find your place

find the goose named Target for the arrow in its back

and the goose named Bulls-Eye for its half a shot-off face

and the goose named Trophy for its mounting on the wall

and the goose named Zip-Tie for the way they brought those cages

and they rounded up them all, all along the misty lakeshore where the grass is slick with shit

and they trucked them to the dark house on the residential block, unpinned the CO_2

and the urban goose time stopped, dropping to the steel cage floor and, double-bagged,

hauled out the door and trucked to the dump to turn to muck in two-ply plastic caskets

by the swamp where they once foraged, duckweed dripping from their chins.

Go there, tiny dragon, let's begin to dream again

of a mountain where the fracking and the coal mines and the prisons all will wane

to the mushrooms and the lichens, to the mildews and the smuts

and tiny dragons' smoky breathing in the elemental dusk will spiral

and meander and knot and twist and coil, corkscrew, weave, and torque

and galaxies will boil and begin the world once more, where humans cannot follow,

being narrowed to the grid, for either on or off it, we are hog-tied to its ego and its id, as prepositions

and conjunctions and, most of all, possessives form our walls and floor and lid.

Little dragon, let us conjure such a place beyond language's checkered tether,

beyond its graph-paper weight, where geese honk up together and fly and fly and fly,

and turbines don't exist there; there's nothing in the atmosphere but living wing and sky.

Go now, lingering dragon. It is time to tell you goodbye

And the rest of us left here on Earth? Let us soften up our edges,

go at night and linger there to vibrate in the sedges with the love song of the frogs,

for if frogs be with us still, then the woodcock's in the bog and he's beeping there,

his beeping not the beeping of relentless human news but the broadcast of his longing,

and he'll rise, and in his slowpoke go-along'ing, bump above the tree line, his dumpy body

singing where blunt feathers meet air's curve, a high-toned lick, a jingle with no words,

then he'll cut his engines, stall himself and, flopping, tumble down,

braid the night like pigtails, hit the ground, stumble to his pink feet, and fluffing,

beep again, and if she comes then, if she doesn't, to us it's all the same,

for the only breadcrumb out of here is the echo that we follow calling sadness by its name,

and in the darkness spot the outlines of all we've lost and done, go home and sleep and wake,

take the blinds off all our windows, and let the mourning come

AIRSTREAMS

Audubon magazine and Audubon.com; Audubon's Birds and Climate Change Report; New York City Audubon's *The eGret*; The Cornell Lab of Ornithology's Merlin app, E-bird app, and AllAboutBirds.com; American Bird Conservancy; The Royal Society for the Preservation of Birds "Nature's Voice" podcast; Lynchburg Bird Club; Franklin Bird Club; Cayuga Bird Club; Road Scholar's Birding in South Texas; *The Genius of Birds* by Jennifer Ackerman; *Gatherings of Angels: Migrating Birds and Their Ecology*, edited by Kenneth P. Able; *On Rare Birds: A Lamentation on Natural History's Extinct and Endangered* by Anita Albus; *Extraordinary Birds: Essays and Plates Rare Book Selections from the American Museum of Natural History Library* by Paul Sweet and Peter Capainolo; *The Book of the Bird: Birds in Art* by Angus Hyland & Kendra Wilson; Prospect Park, Brooklyn; New York State Parks; Finger Lakes Land Trust; Santa Ana National Wildlife Refuge, Estero Llano Grande State Park, Rancho Lomitas, Bentsen State Park, McAllen, Texas; California National Marine Sanctuaries; California State Parks; South Carolina State Parks; Colorado State Parks; Virginia State Parks and Sweetbriar College campus; Pennsylvania State Parks and the Susquehanna River; my Nikon ProStaff 7S binoculars; *Summer World* by Bernd Heinrich; *Winter World* by Bernd Heinrich; Sigurd F. Olson's *The Singing Wilderness*; *Sierra* magazine; *Smithsonian Magazine*; *Anthropocene*; *National Geographic*; EcoWatch.com; Oceana; Waterkeeper; Earth Justice; Center for Biological Diversity; "Summary for Policymakers of the Global Assessment Report on Biodiversity and Ecosystem Services," of the Intergovernmental Science-Policy Platform on Biodiversity and Ecosystem Services Advance Unedited Version, 6 May 2019, by Sandra Diaz, et.al.; International Union for Conservation of Nature's Red List of Threatened Species; "Science Under Siege at the Department of the Interior," by Jacob Carter, et.al., Union of Concerned Scientists, December 2018; "Separation Anxiety: The Perilous Alienation of Humans from the Wild," by Ellen Meloy; *Field Notes from a Catastrophe: Man, Nature, and Climate Change* by Elizabeth Kolbert; *Engaging with Climate Change: Psychoanalytic and Interdisciplinary Perspective*, edited by Sally Weintrope; *Greeting the Angels: An Imaginal View of the Mourning Process* by Greg Mogenson; *Air: The Restless Shaper of the World* by William Bryant Logan; *An Ocean of Air* by Gabrielle Walker;

The End of Night: Searching for Natural Darkness in an Age of Artificial Light by Paul Bogard; *The Cloudspotter's Guide: The Science, History, and Culture of Clouds* by Gavin Pretor-Pinney; *The Oxford English Dictionary*; *The New York Times*; *The New Yorker*; *Harper's Magazine*; *The Atlantic Monthly*; *The Washington Post*; *The Intercept*; *Jacobin*; *The Guardian*; *The Independent*; BBC; NPR; CNN; *Men's Health*; *The Hill*; EarthSky.org; Quartz.com; *Forbes*; *Mother Nature News*; "Here's How America Uses Its Land," by Bloomberg.com; *A Field Guide to the Invisible* by Wayne Biddle; *The Secret Language of the Stars and Planets* by Geoffrey Cornelius and Paul Devereux; *The Hidden Life of Trees: What They Feel, How They Communicate* by Peter Wohlleben; *The Songs of Trees: Stories from Nature's Great Connectors* by David George Haskell; *Simon & Schuster's Guide to Insects* by Dr. Ross H. Arnett, Jr. and Dr. Richard L. Jacques, Jr.; *The Book of Caterpillars: A Life-Size Guide to 600 Species from around the World*, edited by David G. James; *Kill Chain: Drones and the Rise of the High-Tech Assassins* by Andrew Cockburn; LiveScience.com on mustard gas; CraftTechInd.com on performance plastics in automobiles; Jorge Luis Borges; William Butler Yeats; William Shakespeare; James Turrell; Joseph Masco; Henry David Thoreau; Barry Lopez; Maya Angelou; Toni Morrison; Anne Sexton; Abbey Lincoln; Bart Howard; Frank Sinatra; The Fifth Dimension; The Turtles; The Alan Parsons Project; my uncle David Andrews; Inanna and Ereshkigal; Wayne County Historical Society; Lackawanna Coal Mine; Refugee and Immigrant Center for Education and Legal Services; inadequately redacted documents of the U.S. Immigration and Customs Enforcement; Amherst County Virginia Sheriff's Inmate Work Force; "State Impact Pennsylvania," a reporting project of NPR member stations; *The Woman's Dictionary of Symbols & Sacred Objects* and *The Woman's Encyclopedia of Myths and Secrets* by Barbara G. Walker; *The Penguin Dictionary of Symbols* by Jean Chevalier and Alain Gheerbrant, translated by John Buchanan-Brown; *The Book of Symbols: Reflections on Archetypal Images*, edited by Ami Ronnberg and Kathleen Martin; *Symbolic & Mythological Animals* by J.C. Cooper; *Anzu and Ziz: Great Mythical Birds in Ancient Near Eastern, Biblical, and Rabbinic Traditions* by Nili Wazana; *Myths from Mesopotamia: Creation, the Flood, Gilgamesh, and Others*, translated by Stephanie Dalley; The Motherpeace Tarot by Karen Vogel and Vicki Noble; Scott Pruitt, first Secretary of the EPA under Donald Trump; Andrew Wheeler, second Secretary of the EPA under Donald Trump; Ryan Zinke, first Secretary of the Interior under Donald Trump; David Bernhardt, second Secretary of the Interior under Donald Trump; Mike Pompeo, second Secretary of State under Donald Trump; Steven Mnuchin, Secretary of the Treasury under Donald Trump; William Perry Pendley, Deputy Director, Policy and Programs, Bureau of Land Management Exercising Authority of the Director under Donald Trump; Donald Trump; my father; the butterflies, the trees, the bats, the bees, and, most of all, the birds

ACKNOWLEDGEMENTS

For the time and space to write this book, the author thanks Beverly Carter, Molly O'Neill (in memoriam), Hedgebrook, Hambidge Center for the Creative Arts, Kimmel Harding Nelson Center for the Arts, Rensing Center, Soaring Gardens Artists Retreat, Virginia Center for the Creative Arts, and Saltonstall Foundation for the Arts. For her exemplary copy editing, the author thanks Laura L. Washburn. For publishing excerpts of this book, the author thanks The Academy of American Poets' *Poem a Day*, *The Ocean State Review*, *Love's Executive Order*, *Post*, *Anti-Heroin Chic*, *The Ilanot Review*, and *Scoundrel Time*. The author is also grateful to Karyn Kloumann for designing and publishing this book, and for all the work she does as the founder of the radically creative and feminist Nauset Press.

www.ingramcontent.com/pod-product-compliance
Lightning Source LLC
Chambersburg PA
CBHW030515130626
46549CB00007B/3003